CLAIMS
OF
HOME

Poems 1984-2010

DAVID M. KATZ

DOS MADRES PRESS INC.
P.O.Box 294, Loveland, Ohio 45140
www.dosmadres.com   editor@dosmadres.com

Dos Madres is dedicated to the belief that the small press is essential to the vitality of contemporary literature as a carrier of the new voice, as well as the older, sometimes forgotten voices of the past. And in an ever more virtual world, to the creation of fine books pleasing to the eye and hand.

Dos Madres is named in honor of Vera Murphy and Libbie Hughes, the "Dos Madres" whose contributions have made this press possible.

Dos Madres Press, Inc. is an Ohio Not For Profit Corporation and a 501 (c) (3) qualified public charity. Contributions are tax deductible.

Executive Editor: Robert J. Murphy

Illustration & Book Design: Elizabeth H. Murphy
www.illusionstudios.net

Author Photo by Linda Stern

Typset in Adobe Garamond Pro
& Anklepants

Library of Congress Control Number: 2011924154
ISBN 978-1-933675-58-9

First Edition

ACKNOWLEDGMENTS

The following poems, a few of them revised, first appeared in:

The Cortland Review:
> "Borges at the Bat"
> "The Concept of Zero"
> "Glasses and Bridges"

Judaism:
> "Halevi and the Laundress,"
> "Stopping by the Inn"

The New Republic:
> "The Consolation of Philosophy"
> "Pope's Grotto"
> "The Revised Auden" (published as "Collected
> Shorter Poems of W. H. Auden")

Notre Dame Review:
> "Fictional Flaws"

Paris Review:
> "An Ode for William Collins"

Podium:
> "After the Manner of Marianne Moore" (published
> as "At the Editor's Desk")

Poetry:
> "Claims of Home"
> "Satan over Cocktails"

The Raintown Review:
> "Night of the Living Dead"

Shenandoah:
> "Prospero in August"

Southwest Review:
> "After Coleridge"

For Linda, Jacob, and Jesse

TABLE OF CONTENTS 

CLAIMS
OF
HOME

COLLEGE TOUR

The time had come to go to market.
To you, the mileage was ideal.
The cell was buzzing in my pocket.
This trip would be a living hell.

You said your new wife was ideal.
The college was near Baltimore.
Only the divorce was real.
A dog was yapping on the shore.

The college was near Baltimore.
The lights reminded you of Lethe,
The yapping dog upon the shore.
The white Chianti made you sleepy.

You dreamed of going back to Lethe.
Only later did you feel the dread.
The white Chianti made you sleepy.
You slept more soundly than the dead.

Only later did you feel the dread.
The cell was buzzing in my pocket.
You slept more soundly than the dead,
But the time had come to go to market.

STOPPING BY THE INN

After Moses Ibn Ezra

For some reason, the thought of stopping by
To visit them suddenly came to me.
I thought of the place as a wayside inn
Where I could lie down, find temporary
Peace for my journey. I thought I'd find them
Asleep in their beds. Instead, words hovered
In the air amid the headstones, and sleep
Came hard. I asked my father, my mother,
Familiar friends: To what do I owe
Your desertion? Silence lay all about
The stones, and all my dead ones grew quiet.
In that silence they would show me my bed.

CLAIMS OF HOME

How much were you like us? How could we know?
When Ulysses floated into my shop, careworn,
Smudged like a burnt tin can just plunked ashore,
His hood fell away, and I could see his face.
So changed. His eye seemed fixed on final scenes
From so much gazing forward into sealight.
Distraught, he scanned my shelves, peering behind
The floured bread and raisins for his past.
There was nothing back there for him to buy
That could redeem the days when these raw boards
Were native to his smaller feet, when my sweets
Smelled so alluring. The sea was over,
The hard world gone, and there could only be
The end of things: the slow walk home to claims
Of home, uncomprehending glances, Penelope.
But I, who played so little part in them,
Recalled beginnings: How alert the lad
Grew when he saw a cake worth stealing, then
Refrained, canny of consequences, wise
To outcomes even then. A moment passed,
And he was on the shore, a man rigging
Masts and overseeing oars, a chosen one,
One of the larger roughs sailing for Troy.
Yet like the rest, he once had been a boy.

BORGES AT THE BAT

The blind author advances to the plate.
He can hear, if he shuts out the crowd,
The pitcher breathing sixty feet away:
The sound of breath is how he measures men.
They plot the pace and rhythm out together.
The hurler nods in empathy. Ball one.

The late September day contracts to one
Astonishment: the blind man, near the plate,
Taking a practice cut, piecing together
The fragmentary silences of the crowd,
Spitting, toeing the dirt, sensing other men.
He hears the air splitting as he swings away.

The two refuse to give their intentions away,
Surrender ground with a count of one and one.
They might well be a father and son, these men
Who strive for space across a gleaming plate,
The rookie and the writer transfixing the crowd.
Bright eyes, blank eyes, ten thousand eyes together.

The kid gathers his brightest days together
Like an all-star team. Old Borges stays away
From the pitch, misreading signals from the crowd.
They inhale, too late, on a high, hard one
Sliced down the living center of the plate.
The count's now one and two, and these two men

Bear scant resemblance to the other men.
The game's a place where strangers come together.
The umpire contemplates a perfect plate
Out of Plato, bends to whisk the dirt away
With a tiny brush. The hitter wears the number one
On his pinstriped shirt to educate the crowd.

Suddenly, it's night. Borges disdains the crowd,
Hears hardly a hush from the mouths of men.
The silence sets him free to hit like one
Beyond sense. The ball and bat work together
With certain knowledge. The horsehide soars away
Toward the moon: a home beyond the plate.

Home run. The crowd advances to the stairway.
But some, together near the star-struck plate,
Wonder where the two unlikely men have gone.

FICTIONAL FLAWS

> *They could not spare a moment or thought from*
> *the great mental occupation of wishing to live.*
> —Conrad, The Nigger of the Narcissus

The plotters' cabin where you couldn't be.
The character with the character in doubt.
The perfect vividness of the unseen sea.
Digressions forever pulling us out. ...
Conscience-freighted, your tale will soon
Burst caulking in weak seams, revealing flaws
You can't have known; in the shade, a lagoon
Will flash from green to glassy. They make us pause,
Your errant wishes. Yet suddenly you're there,
Shivering in many-motived language,
Wanting only to live. Ruined and spare,
The crew closes in on the end of its voyage,
And steadying hands behind the chorus
Begin to steer Narcissus home to us.

THE SECRET SHARER

I dive into the dream again and breathe
The underwater way, up through a tube.
I seek a passage in a secret book,
A psalter in a chest o'ergrown with weeds.
For all I know the world above is silent.
I pull a hatchet from my belt and swim
To face the lock. It's stronger than it looks
With all that softness growing there around it.
The water slows my arm and yields a stream
Of bubbles. When they clear I see a crack
And swing the axe into a fragile spot.
I toss the broken lock across the floor
As if I were a boy who skips a stone
Across the spangled surface of a lake.
But I turn because the book is what I want,
Not boyhood. Now the time has come to find
The psalm I dove once more to find for you,
My wakeful twin, my shadow on the shore.
The trunk won't give the ghost up easily.
The water's dense and dim beneath the lid.
Yet—look!—some lines in ink are written there:
Oh Lord, release me from this heavy water,
Reveal to me the secret of my dream.

GODS AND MONSTERS

Like a sack of letters I come back to you,
My face as thin as love on onionskin,
My serifs fading, the memories back
To their old tricks again, back to renew
Some glimmer in the mind. But as you spin
And dive in your bubble bath, rise to wash walls
Assiduously, covered with suds, you are a true,
If small, Neptune imbued from head to fin
With all the salty life my long days lack,
Plunging with your trident through the squalls.

Beyond your mythy brink, your brother draws
Funny mechanical monsters. Twirling
A strand of hair, on his belly, he gazes
At the meshing gears, the fierce, archaic jaws,
And pauses. He sees a sadness swirling
Amid any villain's motives. Hounded,
His new Godzilla, fearing the vengeful laws
Of cruel little men, begins hurling
Down Tokyo. Thus, while the Ginza blazes,
The beast himself is the one who's wounded.

Evening deepens; I stumble from your room,
Past the millions of tiny cars, with a sense
Of dazed elation. Some sweetness lingers:
Prismatic color off the bubble, some
Dawnlight of sympathy and ambivalence
Where you were. Then, like jagged streaks of light
That break off after a dive, as the diver comes
Coolly upon a darkness utterly dense,
Consolations disperse. Through my fingers
The gods and monsters rise into the night.

HALEVI AND THE LAUNDRESS

Skin like damp crystal, prismatic eyes revealed
When she drew away her hair's licentious red:
To him she seemed more than something like the sun,
Folding dried clothes, siphoning warmth through her body.
Halting here, a few miles east in Andaluz,
He could have ended his journey. His yearning
Might have bloomed inside her, the long wait for God
Expired in a gasp. It was merely a glance
Before she turned to plunge her arms elbow-deep
To twist the sheets in chilly water and hum
A song the morning birds were humming, a look
To seize in lengths of rhythm, and yet it was
The last remaining obstacle to Zion.

THE CONSOLATION OF PHILOSOPHY
Homage to Salman Rushdie

She threw the lesser muses out
And barred the door. Flame-haired, quick, slim,
She knew what had transfigured him,
Left him passionless and devout.
She vowed she would absorb each doubt,
Drape shadows up and down her system.
"Like a pageant behind a scrim
Where frozen shapes can move about
In slow motion (the ancients caught
Just as their light began to dim),
Memory quickens the unredeemed,"
She said, and the movement of her thought–
The music, more than what she taught–
Sweetened his cell and succored him,
Delivered him from what he'd written,
From history that would burn him out.

But the hard Latin that summoned her
Is unyielding ore. Boethius, a man
About to die, not for Philosophy,
But a swerving regime, tries to remember
Any bright happiness he can;
And she fades, the nurturant genie,
The shadowy erotic dancer....
It was as if all order ran
Out on him, leaving his mind free
To sift through its shiftless splendor.
Silently, the Consolation began
To wriggle from captivity.

THINKING WITH ONE'S FEELINGS

*And poetry is a way of thinking with one's
feelings, anyway.*
　　　—Elizabeth Bishop

The phrase seems clear, but it's hard to get.
Thinking with shadows, with sadness, with anger?
I'm thinking of thinking without regret.

Has the angry sun arisen yet?
The hungry lovers want to linger.
The phrase seems clear, but hard to get.

The morning light caught in my net,
The fluke falling from my finger:
I'm thinking of thinking without regret.

God blesses the ground, the hidden street,
God blesses the maze in the heart of the stranger.
The phrase seems clear, but it's hard to get.

When I was a child, I swam through the net,
Refusing with each breath to surrender.
I'm thinking of thinking without regret.

Perish the thought. Make it forget.
Feel your way in the dark through the danger.
The phrase seems clear, but it's hard to get.
I'm thinking of thinking without regret.

THE GIANT'S HAND

You know we are a unique class, the only three
American writers of our generation who don't have to work.
--Robert Lowell to Elizabeth Bishop, Words in Air

Antwerp
January 2010

Dear –,

Why waste my time resenting them?
She's indecisive, squanders years
As if they were cruzeiros. Cal
Spends winters in the Netherlands
Reading the Nuremburg trials entire.
And as for me? I have to work.
My situation's not unique,
And Flanders blesses anonymity.

*

My skirts are sensible, not manic.
You'd know me: closet alcoholic
With the mouse-grey eyes, the lowly rat
Of envy. Bishop-like coiffure.
I drink with my students, but they never
Drink me in. Late nights in the mirror,
Through a shimmer, I see the little they see
When I smile to check my teeth.

*

Elizabeth, with all her money,
Might still have been a similar
Kind of spinster. I see her
Standing at the edge of a party,
Imported bourbon in her nose,
Watching. She'd turn away from Belgium,
Though. That's where the likeness ends.
She had the talent to be happy.

*

I see us, dear, as girls circling
The campus under rhinestone swaths
Of an Illinois night. If I had turned
To face you in the dark, might it
Have turned out differently?
I've written you each month for years,
Not a note returned to me.
You're someone else entirely.

*

In Samambaia, she shouted LUZ
Into the night. The poet writes
Of the repeated power outages
Elliciting her true complaint
Against the universe. Poor me!
I'd never be so practical
And elegant. I never had
That feeling of entitlement.

*

How did I let you get away?
Better: How could I ever hold you,
Fearful as we both were then,
Hidden as I've been? I loved; it hurt,
And then I turned away from you
Into this hall of mirrors – of letters –
In which I chase my tail and you
All the way to Timbuctoo.

*

And Antwerp, my last stop. This town
Was named for Antigoon, a giant
Who loomed above a nearby river
And took a toll from those who crossed.
If you refused, he'd slice your hand
And toss it in the water. I'm like him,
You see. I want. I want the hand.
I want the hand I cannot have.

*

Landing in Santos, she saw Brazil--
Seized it like a suckling would
A teat, grasping terra firma.
Here the tourist parts the shades
And bathes herself in sunlight. Here
I can't begrudge her anything.
She pays me back with a harbor view,
The view of one who starts to see the world.

Yours ever, —

SATAN
OVER
COCKTAILS

THE REVISED AUDEN

What you were, or are, is no longer clear
To you. This we can learn from the certainty
With which you savage your fine, early self,
Proceeding from lately discovered regulations
Based on a hatred of what you now
Think you sounded like: too many "the's,"
An abuse of self-importance characteristic,
Perhaps, in general, of youth; too many commas,
Now clearly erased because at sixty
You surely know the way the words of forty
Intended. Are you now someone else so clearly?
A different man, of elasticized mind, restrolling
The lacustrine absorptions at Vevey,
Suddenly understanding how misguided you'd been,
In the young, blundering place of your genius?

SATAN OVER COCKTAILS

Gracious, relaxed, ready to concede your point,
Turning to sample just one of the hors d'oeuvres,
Acknowledging another guest, but turning back to you
To discuss your most reasonable assertion
That his most estimable achievements
Are nonetheless limited, he concedes as he eats,
Above all self-contained, and satisfied that,
Having crossed the line into the monstrous,
The unthinkable, all men will come to him.

ALBA

Writing in the morning, just after the birds
Commingle with the crickets, when all sounds subside
A second until they will again persist,
I sense a dangerous presence in the words
This summer house might utter. It might deride
Our sin against stillness, make us desist
From movement altogether, demand paralysis
For admittance to its kingdom's quiet wood.
It might strike from its rooms, forbidding us speech,
All of its voices with a single emphasis,
A constant request for what it knows is good
And what is forever beyond our reach.

HAIKOUM FOR JAMES DEAN

As blank as a stone,
This young tabula rasa,
And bad to the bone.

His passage was clear—
A straight tabula rasa
Up to Salinas.

But nothing was clear
Thirty seconds from Cholame,
Far from Salinas.

He could see the fork
As he floored it for Cholame:
"That guy's gotta stop."

He could see the fork
From his low silver Spyder.
"That guy's gotta stop.

Why can't he see us?"
Shadows blot out the Spyder
As the film slows down.

Though James can't see us,
We see him behind the dash
As the film slows down:

He's blank as a stone,
And blanker behind the dash,
And bad to the bone.

THE CONSPIRATORS

The act was wrong
  and it rankles:
    that old wreck Isaac
      the cataracts so bad

He could only see
  into the dark corners,
    the tent's light-slant
      so dim one son

Seemed the same
  as the other;
    but hairy Esau
      stunk of the fields

And could return with the cut
  of meat old men love,
    in burly arms
      that could lay them to rest;

But here, he sensed,
  was the other,
    thin, slick,
      smooth-skinned one,

The faker, housed
  in the scent
    of his brother's skin,
      bearing the same meat,

Asking for the same blessing.
  The act was wrong
    and it rankles.
      But that old wreck

Isaac knew the game
    from deep in his belly
        as he hung his head
            and allowed himself to be served.

NIGHT OF THE LIVING DEAD

The proper nouns avoid us now.
We parted with particulars
When we left the bodies in the river.

Our pupils are as blank as rivers.
We crave the taste of liver now.
It's our only living particular.

Murder stripped us of particulars,
Made us null, and void as rivers.
We wrap ourselves in pronouns now.

The river knows particulars.

PORTRAIT D'UNE FEMME

The mind has a talent for distortion.
There you are, in your boudoir,
Powder at the ready.
How powerful you are.
How powerful you were.
The mind has a talent for distortion.

The mirror shows something,
But she shows it to you.
The mirror has a talent for distortion.
A man there behind you
Is in the mirror too.
His eyes have a talent for distortion.

The man in the mirror reflects upon you.
The mirror has a talent for distortion.
But is the mirror powerful?
Is the mirror true?
The man in the mirror reflects upon you,
A man with all his distortions.

Who are you really, do you know?
Your mind has a talent for distortion.
The mirror shows something,
But your eyes do too:
There you are, in your boudoir.
You pause before your distortion.

DEATH TAKES A HOLIDAY

At the Dead Sea

All the facts were there, scattered
At the second saltiest sea
Before I fashioned them, saw them as
    A single event.

He was a large child, his folks
Would say—meaning he was swollen
With teasing, meaning he was "fatso"
    To the other kids,

This beached zebra, resplendent
In his one-piece, barber-pole suit.
Traces of flu had seeped through his skin
    From the milky sky

Too powdered for rain or shine.
Of course I could see her coming
From many yards away: Pallid yet
    Unburned, slimmer than

Matter, the malevolent
Girl, picking up her pointed stone
Like a living arrowhead, like her
    Own didactic rune.

Then, sprinting through the shoreline's
Shadows, my native opaque lake
On her left refusing any form
    Of soft reflection,

The lethal sand on her right,
This translucency of a child,
This homunculus on a beeline,
    Papercut waiting

For a finger, would make way
In no time through glinting joggers,
White bra lines, metal pails and shovels
    To the boy, floating

Blissfully on his back on
The solid, saline sea, basting
Like a silent meal under the sun,
    Where nothing is new,

And the fat's already been
Rendered. Let's give him a minute
Of solitude, allow him to breathe
    In his buoyancy,

His boyishness. She will come
Soon enough, in one meager form
Or another, to sink her arrow
    Into his temple;

But since it's in my power
To say, "not now," I will say it
And draw my dense cloak across the rest
    Of my vacation.

THE STANDOFF

Faces in the heavenly choir
Await the minyan's lower fire.
Fish cannot swim, they cannot eat
Until an elder stirs from a seat.

The bears are low, they hate the sky.
They will not let the moon go by.
The whirligig abhors the dark.
The lower hates the higher spark.

No wind, no light, no moon, no air:
A stubborn hush refuses prayer.
They will not say a single thing.
They know they can contain the king.

The miracle is born in anger.
The irate infant will not linger.
No passage in the Father's book
Prepared him for this sullen look.

THE CONCEPT OF ZERO

All we do aspires to what's not there.
   We bang against a door, anticipate a face.
The door swings open to oblige. We stare

Through rows of digits in despair.
   No finger holds the place.
All we do aspires to what's not there.

The Mayans saw zeros fall from the air,
   The bright rings shimmering in space.
A door swung open to oblige their stare.

An egg, an ought, a shell to share
   With ancients who have set the pace.
All we do aspires to what's not there.

Oblong ghosts descend a rising stair,
   Scan the ground for a warm embrace.
Nobody will oblige their stare.

We labor to discount the fear
   That nothing's, really, there to trace—
That all we do aspires to what's not there.
   We bang against a door. We stare.

THE RAV DEFENDS THE LAW

The person who dies first
          must be buried first
                    even though he's poor

And the one you want
          to bury before him
                    gave mightily

To the congregation,
          a man resplendent
                    in his furs.

Yet the one who died first
          must be buried first:
                    the man with fish

On his hands, unshaven,
          who had no dime to give
                    but would give no dime

Even if he had it.
          Here the poor man
                    steps on an untipped scale

Along
          with the rich one
                    naked in his furs.

Here is the line
          You will not cross.
                    Here your arrangement will fail.

It is the law,

you craven burghers,
the one I will beat into you

With my walking stick
should you make
one move to bury this man.

He basks in scented oils.
He will keep.

FACES
OF
AMERICA

CRANE

He drew vast blueprints
Where vanished peoples
Hung like bats from hooks.
The Sumerians,
Itzas, Chingachkook,
Polymath rabbis,
Masters of Talmud:
He fished for nations
With indirection—
Not like Crane, who took
The bridge in his hands
And shook it over
America until
The names and places
Fell to the ground like
Manna at sunrise.

GLASSES AND BRIDGES

"Bridges are big, dumb pieces
    of steel and concrete, and mostly out of mind,
        until one collapses."
        The *Times* writer likens
    the brief span carrying Route 56 over
the Raquette River to a
                                cardiac patient

"studded with instruments." The
    design is to diagnose the animal,
        make the man-made inmate
        solve secrets in its stents
    to "explain how to keep others from falling"
as one fell that rush hour in
                                Minneapolis.

Hovering above matter
    Like a quail quivering over a river,
        Bridges are not glasses.
        Both are mechanical,
    vulnerable; but there the similarity
already stretches its length
                                past credulity.

Bridges are devastated
    By the swaying of their ancient engineers.
        Beasts with thickening waists,
        They ache to come to ground.
    In Brooklyn, men lunched on one while it was built.
Their stable stanchions stress
                                precariousness.

Spinoza's wire-strung lenses
    were, however, neither tense nor tenuous.
      Light as larks, loathe to make
      spectacles of themselves,
   they loom, more heretical than Icarus
Because they survive the sun
                              both had burned to see.

Clear as they are, glasses' flaws
   are obvious to their brothers, the mirrors
      who call them prodigals
      long unaccountable
   to self-reflection or self-knowledge, free birds
Responsible to no face
                              beyond their wearer's.

Borges refers to fame as
   "that reflection of dreams in the dream of an
      other's mirror." Glasses
      avoid love's labyrinths,
   deny the dense motives ensnaring our hearts.
They reflect only briefly,
                              gleam with perfidy,

Lose themselves when we most want
   to find them, having other things on their minds
      than vision's frailty.
      Bright metaphysicians
   enabling vanity, they break readily.
But bridges fall heavily,
                              are hard to replace.

AFTER THE METHOD OF MARIANNE MOORE

It's hard not to imitate
  Who she is, ease yourself in
To the things that remain here,
  The wall of quotes: "Ah…lunch time!"
Or: "Man is a creature whose
  Substance is faith. What his faith
Is, he is." Easy to ape.
  But now, on your desk, new work
Awaits, new words for counting,
  Oddly plumed birds on the hunt
In their quizzical ways to
  Untrammeled inlets for love
And tiny fish. Discarded
  Tissues of reportage, news
Become ink on the finger,
  Whiteout, piles of stray printouts
Left for you to sort. And still:
  "The whole comprises the parts."

FACES OF AMERICA

You think we're all the same. We're not.
Your Uncle Mike is Meryl Streep.
Geronimo's a polyglot.

The family of man grows hot.
The current stew had years to steep.
You think we're all the same. We're not.

You think we came from a single spot?
My hate for you runs cold and deep.
Geronimo's a polyglot.

Cain killed Abe with a single shot.
The road to hell is short and steep.
You think we're all the same. We're not.

We swelter in the melting pot.
My cards are yours to read and weep.
Geronimo's a polyglot.

He speaks with all the tongues he's got.
Our different moms put us to sleep.
We think we're all the same. We're not.
Geronimo's a polyglot.

SECRETS AND LIES

For Mike Leigh

Scene: a scrub-urban birthday barbecue.
Your host, a family photographer,
Serves up a steak that's bigger than the plate
Of the scaffolder, his niece's dimwit beau.
She's fucking him, as they all really know
But act as if they don't. Her mom's rough life,
Seen in her side-long glances, moistening eyes,
Is subject matter for the girl's dull anger,
Her *What about you, Mom, what about you?*
Pan to the fence, up through the whiffle-ball
Meadow rising to the tracks that take you out
To the sticks or to the city. We know more
Than all but one participant can know:
A bomb's about to blow. In a few scenes more
Our host will say what time, piled up like quilts
Above the sleepless maiden's pea, would not
Reveal: Someone was born to someone whom
She shouldn't have been. A mysterious friend arrives.
About her fall the secrets and the lies.

BEFORE HE DIED

Wouldn't you be happy to have written *Lunch Poems*?
No, not to have been Frank O'Hara, not Frank O'Hara
With all that entailed. But to have in your palm
The bright blue and orange semi-square, and open
Again to the scene of sitting at a window at Schrafft's,
The worker with the pneumatic drill visible
But muffled by the glass, as each passerby
Departs like a parasail off Fire Island.
I would be happy to have written that book
And to be slipping it into a raincoat pocket,
Heading expectantly toward Fire Island.

AFTER THE EXTRACTIONS

I won't speak of the loss, but of the gain.
When you get old, they ask you where you've been.
Two teeth are gone that were a source of pain.

For all those years, they fought against the grain,
Dug deep beneath the battlements of skin.
I won't speak of the loss, but of the gain.

Now that they're gone, they won't come home again,
Those silver anchors, stanchions of my grin.
Two teeth are gone that were a source of pain.

They put down roots in snow and in the rain,
And when they left, it hurt me deep within.
I won't speak of the loss, but of the gain.

Divorce is sad. But why should I complain?
When they had to split, the break was clean.
Two teeth are gone that were a source of pain.

Of the three of us, only I remain.
I'm lighter for the journey, hard and lean.
I won't speak of the loss, but of the gain.
Two teeth are gone that were a source of pain.

THIRTEEN APPLES

I

An apple is one.
An orange is one.
An apple and an orange
Are incomparable.

II

Five-and-twenty blackbirds—
And not one apple.

III

When that ripe apple
In its last dapple
Falls, it's autumn,
Not April, for the apple.

IV

Blackbird singing
In the dead of night,
Yearning for an apple.

V

The barrel's filled
With rotting apples.

VI

One bad
Apple don't
Spoil the whole
Bunch, girl.

VII

So much
Depends
Upon
A red
Apple.

VIII

Teacher,
Teacher,
Can
An apple
Secure
An A?

IX

Arms arrive in pairs.
Legs arrive in pairs.
Eyes arrive in pairs.
An apple is not a pear.

X

In Eden,
They say,
The apple
Was really
A fig.

XI

She, the apple of his eyes,
And he, the apple of hers:
The couple saw apple to apple.

XII

I am done
With apple-picking now.

XIII

Your choice of weapons,
Wallace Stevens:
A single blackbird
Or thirteen apples.

PROSPERO
IN
AUGUST

GRAND HUBRIS

Stevens, how Epicurean of you
To contemplate war in the same breath as
Your imagination. I sit here humbled
By the grandeur of your hubris,
Of the ridiculous golden wings
That grace the dark katydid.

It's neither that fall when reality sets in
With its anticipatory agues,
Nor full-throated summer,
When capleted soldiers snore beneath the trees.
It's early spring: You're that surety executive
Exalted on the way to work, clear
Among round golds, sharp greens, breathing an Eden
Of deepest balance, in the season farthest from the war.

DANTE IN FARM COUNTRY

Dust on the van, the return
As if to some late-day paradise
In the late-day light. The rise of the hill
And then the descent, the prospect of the mountains
Distant yet clear through the dust
Of farm country.

A month in the country
Makes for a hard return,
But I want to set it down, before it turns to dust.
In some antechamber of my mind, it was paradise.
I remember, close to departure, a little hill,
And, at some distance, the firm and gentle sweep of mountains.

Charged with more than memories, the mountains
Surged from a power in the land, from country
That could hide all sunlight behind a little hill
And slowly permit it to return
In morning blinks of paradise:
Manure mounds, pinto cows, brilliancies of dust.

The van kicked up the dust.
The clouds began to block the mountains.
Then an overwhelming light, a shard of paradise,
Caught every animal glance in this country
Of the mind, this land of slow returns.
Dante writes of finding a woman on a hill;

Unlike any other lady, she strode that stony hill
Cold to the core. Both he and she are dust,
And still she refuses, and still he vows to return.
Far from these low mountains,
From late-summer light, from farm country,
You can still remember paradise.
I could still remember paradise

In the curl of light around a little hill
As I turned the van from farm country
In a last swirl, a late gleam in the dust.
For a second, the lady stayed with me, as the mountains
Loomed in the mirror; stayed with me as I returned.

Far from those low mountains, from slow-darkening hills,
From the late-summer dust of farm country,
You can still return to paradise.

POPE'S GROTTO

Verse's clarity, verse's vented bitterness
Could not free him from the Cave of Spleen,
Which he then domesticated. Retreating,
Between River and Garden, he dug out
His grotto like a bloodworm, implanted
Cockles in the ceiling, and stayed, reading
In the indifferent light, only in late spring
When the cold departed as a threat
To his twisted bones. To burrow soothed him
As a kind of balm, an antidote to gossip;
It was better not to hear or know
What the gnats were calling you. From here
He held his eroding ground, kindling
The far, high fires of a grand rear guard
Against aguish drafts, numb phalanxes.

AN ODE FOR WILLIAM COLLINS

I

Poor Collins sung the gradual, waiting,
Praying for Eve to arrive. And, while bidding
    For her, sure of failure,
    Found her inadvertently.
Where is she now? Without prayer can she
Make us natural, come without ritual
    In these impatient days?
    Can we find the coolest evening
Here, beyond method, beyond practice
In a most despising age? Like thee, I seek
    An inaccessible wing
    Barely seen in heavy shadow
A few feet past measure, as beloved dusk
Descends. Like thee, I seek an intimacy,
    A capacity to speak
    In a small, evasive voice;
Like thee, the beetle, the leathern bat; like thee
The whisper that ceases, in the evening, to aspire.

II

There you were, twisted, disheveled in the sheets,
A permanent shape of disarray. And then:
    "Smith, do you remember
    My dream?" Your eyes, brightening,
Recalled it as a shared schoolboy glory:
    Your one pathetic gesture,
    Your failed aspiration.
"Yes of course." The talisman produced for him
Sixteen years ago shone again, that burdened
    And unburdened, polished
    And repolished badge

You offered up. "I was walking in a field
Amid the bending grass, when before me
    There arose the straightest,
    Loftiest tree. Suddenly,
Dangerously, I was balanced at the top.
I reached for a stable branch. But the big bough
    Failed with me, let me fall
    To the floor of the wavering field."
You were safe, but uncannily shattered.
Why? "The tree was the tree of poetry."

III

You were weak before the fact, on the verge
Of something overwhelming that could come
    Only with the strength of time.
    You planned tragedies,
But only planned them. You languished,
Borrowed money, fled bailiffs, finished two odes
    In two years, and waned
    Like a dry slice of moon.
I see you, neurasthenic at the end
Of a tortured day, grieving in a dusky light,
    Able just once to forget
    What could never be done.
The night about to come, about to fall
Decisively down, is suspended
    Above signaling shadows;
    Tentative, departing light
Tantalizes, flashes, subsides....
You rise to the large idea of evening,
    A sleepwalker awakened
    At the edge of the woods, condemned
To wait quietly. But you will not rail
Against silence. You are in her service.
    Helplessly you reached for her
    And language never faltered.

AFTER COLERIDGE

The wing of inspiration passes now,
Trailed by its covert shadow, its regrets,
It hints of reminiscence, and we're left
The task of building a city once more.
Was the revolution ever more than waste,
Than plunder of the smallest lives? What stays
Beneath the blue, the peeling, receding waves
Of sunlight? We conjure something that will last
As the brightness flits over the broken roofs;
We turn, and believe we aren't turning. Wings pass
Like the Spirit of France, shadows, old loves. ...
There may never be a way to hold them when
The sun leaves the raw avenues in coolness
As it passes overhead, as if forever, again.

TO SOLOMON IBN GABIROL

Here, where we are less than nothing,
Lower than the reviled thing, the lowest fleas
In the swarm of the lowest, we have only
The closest outcry to mark us,
The babe held close in the coarse blanket,
Our inadvertent, timid meaning.

These small things, as you sit alone
In a late memory of the red sun,
The red wine settled into a clarity
Of mind, are the first solace
Of your wakefulness, the visible breath
Among sleeping comrades.

These things are, for this moment, a meaning
Added to meaning. When the boy once more
Poured clear wine into your cup
From the thick neck of the ewer,
You held the slightest light added
To the abundance of the sunset:

Small meanings added to the large,
Bright feathers onto the pile,
Your talk amid the buzz of comrades.
Confrere, we are both alone now
In a latter section of the night,
Minimalists of a collapsed distance.

Only a single star stares at us,
A tiny scimitar at eye level,
No half-moon beneath the night's eye,
No other light. To make verses, Shlomo,
Is to believe in the one God, to see the source
Rippling toward us in a number.

It's to see, just above the horizon,
The soft star embedded in the law,
The fixed law asleep in starlight,
Vile as we are, the lowest fleas of the swarm.
The desert before us is God, Shlomo,
And only our verses are listening.

PROSPERO IN AUGUST

I

Inside the green road I found solitude,
Delicious solitude, where the words of one man
Do not fall on the anvil of another,
Where the lush saltwater of impulse rises
To quieter consciousness, spouting, in strong,
But measured, waves. Here words can be arranged
In preparation for the great moral dance:
The dancers, gathered perfectly, change hands;
They exchange hearts in the freest flow of feeling;
They clap to meet and quell their passion, while
Their rhythm keeps judicious step beneath
The berry trees, the thick allure of the dusk.
I rose and walked the circling road, its green
Enflamed by my balance and my leisure.

II

I heard my hunters grow satirical,
And saw them hold my nymphs around their waists
Too long to match my music, which took on
A raucous sound in moist and heavy air
That grated with the crickets' legs. This month
Has been a mirror, ripped from what I thought
Would be a seamless time, reflecting power
In its faded state: needles of light that bend
Forever in these waves. ... I tend too much
And then not enough upon Miranda;
Since she has come of age, I would court her
Up to danger, depart at each pleasure,
Hover or leave an angel hovering secure
Between the bedposts, easing my suspense.

III

Until today she grew up entangled
In my magic, her dark eyes searching
Through the ravel of father and nature:
Borne up in my arms as we cut through the waves,
She was a cloud-child beneath my high gaze,
Which was the same to her as the clear sky's
Or the storm's; this island's glinting sand
Was a mystery spread upon her hand.
(Was her father's face the foam upon the sea?)
Her bouncing walk set my vines to circle
Around her, even as she slept, to slow
The darkening in her dreams. No father
Is different, except that I have powers,
And I seek in vain for her glances now.

IV

The interest a city has in its Duke
is mutual: If he engages with it,
Plants his true hatred into its plotters,
Makes it the final symbol of his sex
And of his agony, it will clutch him.
It may kill him, but it will not force him
Into exile. In Milan my craft was hardly
Half-applied; the city would have died amidst
My smoke and incessant numbers. I sought
A balance that could house magic. But the spires
Drew garbled lines across the sky, contempt
Crossed with thunder, beetles scampered between
The thick raindrops I lured. Isolation's
Whirlpool pulled us: This island then arose.

V

Solid light out of liquid, I thought,
Soft yellow-pink and turquoise pounded out,
Ascending from the deepest streams of blue. ...
Released from extremes, color's rarest strains
Emerge, and make a god of men who can
Perceive them. Had I not arranged it all?
In Milan, I wished to be the only man,
The magic man inside the head of state.
No doubt I wore this as a badge upon
My wound. No doubt I signaled silently
To my brother: Replace me. For I lived
To animate the sky; to rule both coarse
Caliban and airy Ariel; to weave
This silken light inconsequentially.

VI

Rain pierced the darkness when we first sailed here
And scored it with little holes, forming a net
Which could draw us up from any bottom.
None could now endanger the protector
And his daughter, asleep in starry skeins.
When I awoke it was to my second
Freshness, tempered by senses that had courted
Such new air before, risen with the same scent,
Yet not purely alone. Again the citron trees
Burgeoned, though I knew them from afar;
The birds, already named, could be orchestrated.
Dialogues began. A later, softer god
Might gently preside, rather than create.
For a bright interlude, he might suffice.

VII

All self-contained in wishful sleep, all sewn
With playful filigree, all irritants
Enclosed in bubbles, all failures dissolving
In drowsy laughter, I let the god arise
In living stories. Each night I met him
In my book, hatching elements anew;
He moved my hand and mapped the air
Above the island, how breezes made the waves
Move themselves, the many ways that spirits
Could collide. Where was satisfaction found?
In this grove. Conflict? In that curved inlet.
By day, in a path I thought predestined,
I would meet him in a hare's black pupil,
And from my own smile gain satisfaction.

VIII

The paths grew intricate. Cross-hatched in dust,
Pressed through pine bushes, in cells below
The sea, the lines were drawn to my intent.
Now, I see night's first star begin to pierce
Another pattern. Underfoot, these white rocks
Seem spines of a receding galaxy
Whose limits my companion first knew.
Become fierce and unseen, he would lead me
Into larger action. I must have hands
To bear my emptiness back to Milan,
And to trace the likeness of the woman
Taken before Miranda knew a mother;
Old citizens must sail toward a grief
Long woven in this island's low laughter.

IX

I remember godlight in the wineglass
Poured before our vows, the hush alighting
On her sinewy outline. How that rhythm
Returns! As the lovers, we opened the dance
And merged with the celebrants, the glowing core
Of that moment. That quick light, gathering up
The god in us both, begins to dart above
Miranda's face, flickers against the walls
Of her dark room, enkindling my unclaimed
Widower's sorrow. Alone, actionless,
Unable to mourn, I need a storm to break
This summer's calm; no longer can I feel
That nuptial power, its discordant force
That yet holds the globe together.

X

They will come, borne on a broken sea
That had been sleek, and bronze to its bottom.
Their greatest bewilderments will replace
Inept surety with truer confusion;
Men driven to jest, they will again be
My jesters. They will come as figures
In a dream, who, motiveless in themselves,
See their actions swim across an unfurled map,
Moved by unseen intentions. Blundering
Up out of the deep, the deep of trapped sighs
And thwarted laughter, beneath pretense,
They will buckle and fall flat on this shore.
They are the agents of my uncertain
Release, the subjects of my last magic.

ABOUT THE AUTHOR

David M. Katz's poems have appeared in *Poetry, The Paris Review, The New Republic, Shenandoah, Southwest Review, Notre Dame Review* (both print and online), *The Cortland Review* and *Podium*, the online publication of the 92nd Street Y. His first book of poems, *The Warrior in the Forest*, was published by House of Keys.

A journalist and editor, he lives in New York City and is New York Bureau Chief of CFO Publications.